My House Is Singing

POEMS BY Betsy R. Rosenthal

ILLUSTRATED BY Margaret Chodos-Irvine

HARCOURT, INC.

Orlando   Austin   New York   San Diego   Toronto   London
Manufactured in China

ONE GIANT HUG

It's not new in town,
hoping to make a first friend.
It's been around.

It never picks a fight with me
or pokes at me
or calls me names.

It doesn't go places without me;
I know where to find it
every day.

It keeps me warmer than a coat,
drier than an umbrella,
and safer than a good luck charm.

It gives me corners to hide in,
closets to whisper in,
and quiet places where I can think.

It's one giant hug,
wrapping itself around me,
no matter what.

It's my house.

HEATER

On winter mornings
my house
blows and blows
on its rooms
to keep warm.

MY BEDROOM
SLIPPERS

They lie
beside my bed,
waiting
for my icy toes
to wake them up.

MAGNETIC SCRAPBOOK

From Niagara Falls to the Golden Gate,
I'll take you on a tour.
It's all up on our scrapbook:
the refrigerator door.

THE SMOKE DETECTOR

Why is it that
whenever I make my toast
a little crispy,
you tell on me?

for the all-you-can-eat buffet.

Black dots hurry single file up the wall to the counter

ANTS!

IN THE LAUNDRY ROOM

On cold days
I pull open the dryer's mouth
to feel its warm breath
while the clothes
are still tumbling.

SOCK EATER

On laundry days
my mother says
the dryer is a crook.

It's all because
a sock is gone—
the one the dryer took.

I tell my mom she shouldn't
let the dryer
see us eat.

It's sure to munch
a sock or two
because it craves a treat.

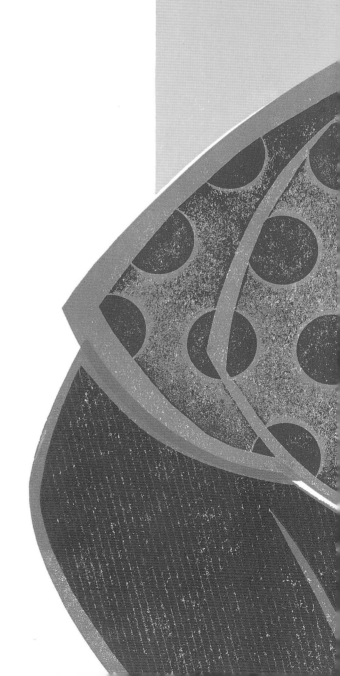

THE INTERRUPTER

Just when I've got things to say,
it starts that ring-ring-ringing song.
When Mom and I have games to play,
that ringing song gets in our way.
Can't it stop for just one day?
Always when the time's all wrong,
and just when I've got things to say,
it starts that ring-ring-ringing song.

MOM'S PIANO RULE

She doesn't mind our fingers tickling
or sliding up and down the keys.
Mom has just one simple rule:
"No banging on the ivories, please!"

OUR LOST-AND-FOUND COUCH

First we checked beneath her skirt,
and swept away the dust and dirt.
Then we fluffed the cushions up
and found an ancient sipper cup,
the missing candlestick from Clue,
a hippo from our plastic zoo,
and Barbie's long lost silver shoe.

ME VS. VACUUM

When the vacuum
starts its roaring,
I start calling
to be heard.

Dad can't hear me;
he keeps pushing.
Vacuum swallows
every word.

I try shouting
even louder.
Now it's rumbling
by my feet.

Vacuum cleaner
sucks my voice up.
Vacuum cleaner's
got me beat.

When I walk up and down the halls,

I smile at faces on the walls.

OUR
PICTURE
GALLERY

It almost seems like they can see—

they always smile right back at me.

THE KITCHEN'S PERFUME

Cookies baking,
hot dogs roasting,
onions frying,
buns are toasting.

Room to room,
through solid walls,
good smells wander
down the halls.

MY HIDEAWAY

In our house there are some stairs
and up those stairs there is a room
and in that room there is a door
and through that door there is one more.
And just behind that my-size door
there is a place where I can store
my rocks, my bugs, my diamond rings,
and lots of other private things.

But I won't tell you any more
about what hides behind that door
'cause if I did it wouldn't be
a place with secrets
just for me.

OUR WEARY OLD ROOF

Its armor, worn thin,
pierced through in places
from so many stormy battles,
has finally surrendered to the enemy...

drip

by

drip.

STUBBORN BACK DOOR

You're stuck shut today.
No matter how hard I tug and I pull,
I won't get my way.
You're stuck shut today.
I can beg you and scold you,
but nothing I say
will get me my way.
You won't open up.
You're
stuck
shut
today.

The lightbulb blinked as if to say, "I just can't last another day."

THE STUFF PLACE

It's a home
for bags of too-small clothes
and baby toys to give away,
for dusty books my parents say
they'll read someday,
for boxes full of old paint cans,
rusty tools and broken fans,
buckets and shovels,
the Slip 'n Slide,
and all the bikes we hardly ride.
I've heard that garages
are built for cars.
There's never been room
for one in ours.

OUR NEW DOORBELL

We never fixed our doorbell,
but we'll hear you just the same,
because we got a new one—
a doorbell with a name.

Our new bell jumps and barks
and fetches lots of things.
He's really much more fun
than a bell that only rings.

WORN OUT

Faded by sun,
coming unraveled,
our front mat is tired
from welcoming
so many feet.

HALLWAY CHAIR

The chair sits by the front door,
enjoying the open air
and dreading its 3:30 burial
under backpacks,
lunch boxes,
sweaters,
and Mom's purse.

THE GROWING TABLE

Our dining room table

g r o w s l o n g e r

when relatives come.

It shrinks
after
they
leave.

COUCH'S SURPRISE

By day
I sit on her and rest,
and then at night
when there are guests,
we help her off
with her disguise
of velvet cushions—
there she lies:
stretching out
from foot to head,
she turns from couch
into a bed.

FIREPLACE SHOW

When snapping flames
call my eyes to the show,
I fall under the spell
of the flickering glow.

ROCKING CHAIR

You're better than a lullaby.
You rock me so quietly.
You rock my eyes closed.
You rock my body calm.
You rock me into sweet dreams.

MY HOUSE'S NIGHT SONG

Listen closely.
Can you hear?

Heater whooshing out
warm air.

Blinds flapping.
Floors creaking.

Clocks ticking.
Faucet leaking.

Dishwasher clicking.
Pipes pinging.

Listen closely.
My house is singing.

COCOON

I'm wrapped up in my
flowered spread,
ready for
the night ahead.

Through the blinds
are hints of moon;
a million stars
will be here soon.

I hum myself
a gentle tune,
and drift to sleep
in my cocoon.

For Dave, Adam, Sara, and Joel,
who share my singing house with me —B. R. R.

For Clare —M. C.- I.

Library of Congress Cataloging-in-Publication Data
Rosenthal, Betsy R.
My house is singing/by Betsy R. Rosenthal; illustrated by Margaret Chodos-Irvine.
p. cm.
Summary: Poems about some of the things that are in a child's home, from furniture and lightbulbs to the cocoon
of a flowered bedspread, and the feelings associated with them.
1. Children's poetry, American. 2. Household appliances—Juvenile poetry. 3. House furnishings—Juvenile poetry.
4. Dwellings—Juvenile poetry. 5. Home—Juvenile poetry. [1. House furnishings—Poetry. 2. Dwellings—Poetry.
3. Home—Poetry. 4. American poetry.] I. Chodos-Irvine, Margaret, ill. II. Title.
PS3618.O8395M9 2004
811'.6—dc21   2002153855
ISBN 0-15-216293-3

First edition
A C E G H F D B

The illustrations in this book were created using a variety of printmaking techniques on Rives paper.
The display type was created by Jane Dill.
The text type was set in Stone Sans.
Color separations by Colourscan Co. Pte. Ltd., Singapore
Manufactured by South China Printing Company, Ltd., China
This book was printed on totally chlorine-free Stora Enso Matte paper.
Production supervision by Sandra Grebenar and Pascha Gerlinger
Designed by Judythe Sieck